50 Exciting Ways to Use a Builder's Tray

ACKNOWLEDGEMENTS

Written by: Helen Bromley

Illustrated by: Peter Scott

Produced & Published by: Lawrence Educational Publications
Unit 21 Brookvale Trading Estate, Moor Lane,
Birmingham, West Midlands B6 7AQ.
Telephone: 0121 344 3004   Fax: 0121 344 3600

© Lawrence Educational 2002

ISBN: 1-903670-15-2

First printed: October 2002
Re-printed: February 2004
Second re-print: December 2004
Third re-print: September 2005
Fourth re-print: March 2006

Introduction

In this book you will find numerous suggestions for using a builder's tray, or 'tough spot,' as they are sometimes known. These trays provide enough space for several children to play around, encouraging personal, social and emotional development. On a practical note, they are long lasting, relatively cheap and easy to obtain, and offer opportunities for both indoor and outdoor play. Their shape and proportions mean that they can be used to contain a wide variety of play materials, including paint and water.

The ideas in the book cross all curricular areas and you will need to make decisions about your particular focus when choosing one of the activities to try out. All the activities suggested offer invaluable opportunities for developing knowledge, understanding and skills in the area of Communication, Language and Literacy and provide enjoyable, purposeful opportunities for children to talk and learn together.

Please remember that a period of exploratory play should be integral to all the activities in this book, before the children are set any specific tasks. It is likely that this period of exploratory play will be repeated, not once, but several times, giving the children a rounded view of the resources and experiences that are available in that particular activity.

The list of suggestions in this book is not intended to be exhaustive, and of course you may begin with an idea suggested here and take it and develop it in your own way. It is also important for practitioners to remain open to the children's own ideas, so be aware that they may have suggestions of their own to offer.

Have fun!

Helen Bromley

Hints and Tips.

✓ Once an activity has been set up, allow it to remain in the setting for at least a week, so that all children get the opportunity to experience the activity, and to return to it to further develop their play. This is far more beneficial than if they are only allowed 'one turn' of the activity.

✓ Be sensitive to the fact that some children night not like the more messy activities suggested here. Allow them to watch other children, rather than insisting that they must handle materials, or toys that they find unpleasant.

✓ Provide aprons for the more messy activities so that children feel that they can be really 'hands – on' without worrying about their clothes.

✓ Make sure that the children know that there are facilities nearby where they can wash their hands.

✓ Take a selection of photographs of children using the tray. If possible, enlarge them to A3 size and laminate them. Keep them near the tray. Explain to the children that you are going to play a game called 'catch me'. The adults in the setting are going to look to see if they can 'catch' the children using the tray, playing like the children in the photographs. This activity can often help to pre-empt behaviour problems, and children really enjoy being caught.

Activity 1

The Living Island.

Resources:
Newspaper, chicken wire, multi-purpose compost, and a variety of quick growing seeds – this could include mustard and cress, alfalfa, grass seed and mung beans. A hand held plant sprayer is also very useful.

Process:
Screw up some newspaper into large balls and build a mound in the builder's tray. Leave a margin around your 'island' so that this can represent the sea. Covering the newspaper mound with chicken wire will give it stability, but is not absolutely necessary. (A fine mesh pea and bean net would serve a similar purpose.)
When you have done this, pour multi purpose compost all over the mound, to create your island. Then sprinkle a variety of seeds over the compost. You will now need to water the island. Use the hand held plant sprayer, and make sure that the entire island is damp. Encourage the children to participate in watering the island on a regular basis.

Very soon it will start to grow – creating a living small world, indoors or out. You now need the island to be inhabited. This can be achieved in a variety of ways. Use animals, e.g. dinosaurs, or play people. (Or both, for increased dramatic possibilities.) Encourage the children to use the island for small world play.

Further possibilities:
Keep a photographic diary of the development of the island and make into a book, or display the photographs on the wall.
Make maps, guides and postcards for the island.
Keep a diary of 'our adventures on the island'.
Tape-record some of the stories that the children make while they are playing.

If you are using Maurice Sendak's 'Where The Wild Things Are', then you could use your small world as The Land of The Wild Things. Encourage the children to draw some wild things of their own to live on the island.

The Ice Mountain

Resources:
Several bags of ice cubes (readily obtainable from the frozen food section of most supermarkets.), cornflour, salt, glitter, soap flakes, bubbles, food colouring small toy animals (e.g. polar bears, penguins, etc.)

Process:
Sprinkle cornflour all over the base of the builder's tray. This does not need to be a thick layer of cornflour – you will get a good effect with just a light sprinkling. Then, tip the bags of ice cubes into the tray, on top of the cornflour. The effect is most striking if you pile them up in the centre of the tray, so that they resemble a mountain.

You can then choose to involve the children in making additions to this environment, so that it changes and develops over time. Encourage the children to predict what will happen when they make the changes to the ice mountain. Make sure that they have plenty of opportunity to stand and watch the ice melting and colours changing, as well as to talk about what they have observed. The ice will naturally fascinate the children and you need to recognise that they will want to handle the materials.

Sprinkle salt over part of the mountain, watch what happens and listen carefully!

Pour two different food colourings (yellow and blue are good ones to choose) over two different parts of the ice mountain.

Sprinkle glitter over the ice and into the cornflour.

Blow bubbles across the ice and into the builder's tray.

Add small arctic or Antarctic animals.

Further possibilities:
Freeze a selection of small items (petals, leaves, tiny beads or buttons etc) in an ice cube tray and mix these ice cubes in with the others.

Freeze a selection of coloured ice cubes and add to the ice mountain.

Freeze a large block of ice (in a Tupperware box, plastic glove, balloon or similar) and hide this in the middle of the ice mountain. Watch the children's reactions as it appears, and then disappears again.

Keep a record of what happens on Ice Mountain. This may be by photographs or children's drawings.

Collect vocabulary to describe the ice mountain, and display on cards with the photographs and children's drawings.

Activity 3

Desert Island Adventures

Resources:
Sand, water, shells, pebbles, driftwood, twigs, hanging basket moss, play people, etc.

Process:
Use the damp sand to build an island in the middle of the builders' tray. Add driftwood, pebbles, moss and shells to create a 'desert island' environment. Put the play people on the island. Finally, gently pour water into the builders' tray. Your play people are now effectively marooned!
Encourage the children to play with the small world – listen to their stories, interactions and conversations. This will give you some ideas of how to develop the activity further.

Further possibilities:
This mini environment offers endless possibilities for problem solving activities and for promoting both narrative and non-narrative writing. Here are a few suggestions. You and the children may think of many more.

Problem solving:
Building a place for the people on the island to live
Making them a raft or boat, so that they can sail home.
If you make two small islands in the tray, children can build a bridge between them.

Writing:
Writing diaries of the characters and their adventures on the island.
(This activity will be enhanced by use of a camera)
Sending postcards from the island
Composing help messages to put in a bottle
Making maps
Writing names in the sand
Making a list of rules for people that visit or inhabit the island.

Activity 4

Jurassic Park

Resources:
Ferns, miniature conifers, largish rocks, pebbles, hanging basket moss, toy dinosaurs, books about dinosaurs.

Process:
Cover the base of the builder's tray with the moss; add ferns and conifers to create a very prehistoric looking environment. Position the rocks throughout the 'land'. Add the dinosaurs. You might also wish to add some people – this may not be historically correct, but it will change and add to the story potential of the environment.

Encourage the children to play with the small world. Observe their interactions and give time to listening to their conversations. You might be surprised about he knowledge that they are able to demonstrate through playing with the toys. Listen for mathematical, scientific and historical vocabulary. Take note of the questions that the children ask each other.

Spend time planning questions to ask the children. Try to avoid those such as 'How many dinosaurs can you see?' Instead build on what you hear and use questions to move the children's thinking on, rather than to test them.

You might wish to keep some of the following books near to your dinosaur world:
Harry and the Dinosaurs by Ian Whybrow
Dinosaur Roar
Saturday night at The Dinosaur Stomp
Time Tunnel, by Arthur L'Hommedieu
Dinosaurs, by Bert Kitchen, Cambridge Reading Scheme.

Further possibilities:
Why not make a dinosaur spotter's guide with the children? They could either draw pictures or take photographs.

This activity will be enhanced if you add and take away different types of dinosaur on different days.

Encourage the children to help look after the plants in' Jurassic Park'. Look for pictures of prehistoric environments in books or on the Internet. How does theirs compare?

Change the weather conditions in Jurassic Park by spraying with water from a hand held plant sprayer.

Activity 5

Walking through the Jungle

Resources:

A variety of tropical, leafy house plants of a suitable size, greengrocer's grass or hanging basket moss, gravel, pebbles, water, toy jungle animals, hand held plant sprayer.

Process:

Line the builder's tray with either moss or green grocers grass, or a mixture of both. Position the pebbles and gravel in various areas – you might like to create a path with the gravel. Add the houseplants to create a jungle scene. Spray with water so that droplets form on the leaves of the plants and the gravel and pebbles are wet ands shiny.
Add the toy animals. You now have your own jungle.
You might wish to create a pool in the jungle by filling a shallow dish with water and placing it in amongst the pebbles, moss and plants.

Further possibilities:

Why not use your small world to write new versions of favourite stories? For example, read Brown Bear, Brown Bear by Eric Carle to the children.
Using this format you could create your own book, using the model animals. It might go something like this 'Blue Parrot, Blue Parrot, what do you see?' 'I see green crocodile looking at me.' 'Green Crocodile, Green Crocodile what do you see?' I see stripy snake looking at me.' 'Stripy snake stripy snake what do you see.' Etc., etc.,
We're Going on a Bear Hunt also provides an invaluable model. This could readily be changed to feature any jungle animal, and your homemade environment could replace those in the original book. (uh, oh vines – twisty, twirly vines, etc.)

When the book is made, keep it by your small world so that children can re-act their own story, using the props available.

Activity 6

I don't like spiders and snakes!

Resources:
Shredded paper (the sort sold for pet bedding is ideal), toy spiders and/or snakes. These should be in a variety of shapes, colours and sizes.

Process:
Fill the builder's tray with shredded paper, piling it high into a mound. Bury your spiders and snakes in the mound and let the children explore. This activity encourages all sorts of discussion and provides some wonderful opportunities for developing mathematical vocabulary.

Further possibilities:
This activity makes an excellent context in which to promote personal, social and emotional development. Children will need to respect each other's fears and feelings. Their attitudes towards the activity will obviously vary greatly, from one child to another.

Change the selection of hidden reptiles and insects.

Work alongside children to sort and classify their finds. Help them record their finds in a variety of ways.

Give the children thick paper or thin card cut into a spiral, and encourage them to write down their feelings about snakes. Attach these by a long thread and display above the shredded paper world, suspended from the ceiling so that they twist and move around.

Activity 7

A Cave for a Bear

Resources:
Newspaper, chicken wire, wallpaper paste.
An inhabitant for the cave – perhaps a bear!

Process:
Because of their virtually indestructible nature, builder's trays make an excellent base for paper mache constructions. Chicken wire provides a stable base on which to support the paper mache and can be readily moulded into a wide variety of shapes.

For this activity take a large piece of chicken wire and mould it into the shape of a cave. Place it in the builder's tray. Mix the glue and tear the newspaper into thin strips. With the children's help cover the chicken wire in several layers of newspaper and glue. Allow it to dry. At this stage you might wish to add to the shape of the cave by attaching screwed up balls of newspaper to the basic cave structure with sellotape and covering with more layers of paper mache. This will give the cave a rocky appearance.

When the glue is completely dry, you will need to add colour to the cave. You might decide to paint it, or to cover it in torn tissue paper, and wash with watered down PVA glue. This gives a very shiny appearance.

When your cave is finished you will need an inhabitant. If you have been reading We're Going on a Bear Hunt with the children, then place a bear in the cave. The children could write him letters of apology, or suggest ways that he might improve security for his home, so that uninvited guest cannot just walk straight in.

Add other bear figures so that the bear has some friends (he appears very lonely in the story).

The children can then make up their own adventures in and around the cave.

Further possibilities:
Once you have made the cave with the help of the children, it will provide you with an invaluable resource for small world play for some time to come. Change the inhabitant – a dragon would be a wonderful addition to the cave, or a group of Playmobil people. Ask the children for their ideas.

You could use the cave as a basis for shared writing. Write the story of the dragon's adventures. Take your time, writing a small piece of the story each day over the period of a week, so that children have the opportunity to play with the cave and thus get new ideas to contribute to the writing sessions. Each shared writing session does not need to be long, but will offer the children an invaluable opportunity to see what it is that writers need to do and to make links between spoken and written language.

Make other environments from papier mache – a volcano, for example, or a small mountain range. You could also make a hill, and use it for Jack and Jill – or the Grand Old Duke of York and his 10,000 men!

Activity 8

Soap Flakes and Sculptures

Resources:
Boxes of soap flakes, water, a variety of whisks.

Process:
Tip the soap flakes into the builders' tray. (You can experiment with different ratios of soap flakes to water) Add water gradually. With the children, whisk up the water and the soap flakes. Try a variety of whisks – which one do the children prefer – why?
What changes do the children notice taking place?

After a while (during the space of a day) the whisked soap flakes will become malleable and the children will be able to form them into sculptures that will dry further overnight, until they are quite hard.

Encourage the children to form abstract shapes with the whisked flakes. Can they think of a name for their sculpture?

There will be space in the builders' tray for several individual sculptures or one collaborative effort.

Take photographs of the finished results and make a sculpture gallery. Type up the process for parents and carers so that they can repeat the activity at home with their children.

Further possibilities:
Add food colouring or glitter, or both, to the soap flake and water mixture.

Give the children a word to explore for their sculpture theme. Can they make a happy sculpture for example – what do they think a 'peaceful sculpture might look like?

Collect pictures of sculptures in a variety of forms so that the children can see the work of other artists.

Try this activity outside!

Activity 9

Crazy Cous Cous

Resources:
Enough uncooked cous cous to cover the bottom of the builders' tray completely.

Process:
Pour the cous cous over the bottom of the builders' tray.
Encourage the children to use their fingers to make marks in the grains.

Further possibilities:
Use this is an opportunity for the children to practice writing their names.
It offers a comfortable, stress free environment for writing practice,
as none of the marks are permanent, and their attempts can easily be rubbed out!

Practice individual letters or groups of letters, key words, etc. With this type of activity it is very important that the children feel comfortable enough to take risks. Praise what they do correctly.

You might wish to put children with a partner for this activity. Put those who find letter formation easy, with those who find it more difficult. In this way children can learn from and support each other.

Encourage the children to make a variety of patterns in the cous cous - wavy lines, zigzag lines, etc.

Use more than one finger at a time to make multiple tracks through the grains.

Activity 10

Spaghetti Junction

Resources:
Cooked spaghetti, food colouring, and a variety of kitchen utensils.

Process:
Cook the spaghetti. If you would like to colour it, either add food colouring to the cooking water (you will need to add quite a lot), or add food colouring to the pile of plain cooked spaghetti. Provide a variety of implements for the children to use – spoons – forks – pasta servers – tongs – etc.

Encourage the children to handle the spaghetti with their bare hands as well as with the cooking implements. What does the spaghetti feel like? What does it remind them of?

Further possibilities:
Change the type of pasta that you use – tagliatelle or linguine will provide a similar but slightly different experience.

Provide a variety of pastas (including red and green pasta) mixed together. This will offer further opportunities for talk and discussion.

Keep some uncooked pasta near the activity – both dried and fresh if possible. Talk to the children about the changes that take place when the pasta is cooked. What happens? Why does the cooked pasta change texture and colour?

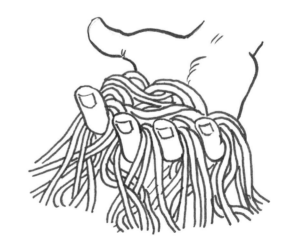

Three Billy Goats Gruff

Resources:

Greengrocers' Grass (or any green material), pebbles, strip of blue fabric, three toy goats, troll, bridge (the sort available from a train set would be just fine.)

Process:

The tale of the hungry goats that overcome the fierce troll is a very popular choice for use in early years settings. You can recreate the story scene very easily in the builders' tray, offering the children to revisit, re-enact and interpret the story through play.

Line the builders' tray with either the green grocers grass or the green fabric. Position the blue fabric across the tray to represent the stream, in which the troll lives. Put the bridge over the stream, with the troll nearby. Place the goats on one side of the stream – the stage is now set for the story to take place.

Keep a copy of the Three Billy Goats Gruff nearby, but make sure that the children feel that they can improvise on the original and create new stories of their own. They might like to consider whatever happened to the troll…. That would be a story in it's own right!

Further possibilities:

Use the builders' tray to set up other story or song scenes. Old MacDonald's Farm would be a good one to do. Keep the song   lyrics nearby, so that the children can sing along as they play. Other stories might include The Gingerbread Man and The Three Little Pigs. The children could be involved in making the props and setting the scene.

Activity 12

The Archaeological Dig

Resources:

Enough sand to completely fill the builders tray, brushes (pastry brushes or short handled thick paint brushes are ideal), some home made fossils (see below), magnifying glasses, trays to collect 'finds', small plastic bags to keep finds in, shells, pieces of crockery, keys, coins, etc. and have some plasticene and plaster of Paris available.

Process:

If you want to include some home made fossils in your dig, then this is what you need to do:
Rollout some plasticene so that it is about 2cm thick. Cut into circles. With the children make prints in the plasticene with shells, coins, keys, in fact anything that will make an indentation in the modelling material. Make a cardboard collar for the plasticene and wrap it around it, fastening with a paper clip. Mix the plaster of Paris and pour into the paper collar. Leave to set. When dry, remove the plasticene base and the paper collar. You will now have a homemade fossil.

Place the homemade fossils in the builders' tray, along with any other objects that you wish to add. Old coins, pieces of broken crockery (carefully sanded down for safety) interesting stones and keys all make for interesting finds.

Give the children the opportunity to work with the dig, carefully brushing away the sand from their finds.
They might wish to bag up their finds and give them labels.

Further possibilities:

Keep a book near to the dig so that children can record their finds. Add new objects over a period of time so that children are motivated to return to the activity.
This activity offers opportunities for a wide variety of discussions. You might wish to make a time line with the children, so that they can make decisions about how old they think their finds are.
A museum role-play area would be a good accompaniment to this activity.

Activity 13

The Rock Pool

Resources:
Shells, a sprinkling of sand, pebbles, rocks, model fish, crabs, etc.

Process:
Place a sprinkling of sand at the bottom of the builders' tray. Add the rocks, pebbles, shells and toy sea creatures. Carefully pour water into the tray so that the environment looks like a rock pool.

Allow the children to explore the pool and to play with the creatures, making up stories.

Further possibilities:
Read the stories 'One World' by Michael Foreman or 'Sally and the Limpet' by Simon James to the children. Such quality children's literature will enhance their play as they will be able to appropriate language from the books and use it in their play. The plots of the stories will also give children new ideas for stories.

The children might like to bring in shells from home to add to the rock pool.

Activity 14

Grains and Pasta

Resources:
Grains, pulses and pasta shapes. Sieves, tea strainers, chopsticks, tweezers, spoons (including slotted spoons) tiny containers, cork tiles.

Process:
Place a mixture of grains, pulses and pasta in the builders' tray – enough to cover the base.
Encourage the children to investigate and sort the grains by a variety of means, using tweezers, chopsticks, sieves etc.

Further possibilities:
Let the children choose a selection of grains and pasta that they find interesting. Talk to them about their choices.
Have them lay out the chosen piece on a cork tile and arrange in patterns or use to make simple pictorial representations.
Use tiny containers (e.g. coke bottle lids) to collect some grains – tip them out onto their tile. Can they estimate how many objects are there?

This type of activity helps develop the fine motor control that children need when it comes to the secretarial aspects of the writing process.

Diggers and Trucks

Resources:

Grain, rice etc. Diggers, fork lift trucks, tipper lorries, etc. A selection of containers to be filled.

N.B If you do not feel comfortable using foodstuffs for play, then the small sized coloured gravel readily available in aquatic centres is an excellent alternative.

Process:

Fill the builders' tray with grain or gravel. Add the trucks. Allow time for exploratory play. Observe the children carefully to see where their interests lie. Some of them will want to make stories; others will work intently to use the trucks to fill the containers. Some will want to push the trucks and diggers through the grain to make patterns and noises.

Further possibilities:

Encourage the children to make estimates about the volume of the various containers – can they guess how many shovelfuls of grain a particular box will hold?

Listen to the noises that the vehicles make in the grain. Cut out a variety of 'noise' bubbles. Invite the children to write down the noises that they hear. The beauty of this activity is that they really can't spell the noise incorrectly…. Collect the bubbles and make a display of the noises.

Add some Bob the Builder and Wendy figures to the tray. You will probably find that you will be inundated with children wanting to play

Activity 16

Making Tracks

Resources:
Toy vehicles (preferably ones that can be washed easily- small plastic cars are ideal).
A selection of paints of various colours, trays for the paint.

Process:
Put a selection of paints into the trays. Experiment with a variety of thickness. Invite the children to choose a vehicle and run it through one of the paint trays – then drive it across the builders' tray. They can repeat this process as many times as you like.
Look at the various patterns made by the tyres.
Can they tell which vehicle made which tracks?
How does the thickness of the paint affect the tracks?
Who can make the longest track before the paint runs out?
What happens when a blue track runs over a yellow one, for example?

Further possibilities:
Repeat this activity on coloured sugar paper for a permanent version. They make a lovely display.
Cover the base of the builders' tray with a thickish paint, and run cars across it, so that the children see the effect in reverse. What is the same? What is different?

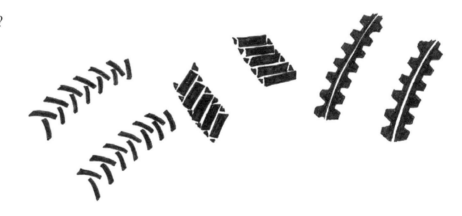

Bubble Printing

Resources:

Powder paint, coloured inks or food colouring, washing up liquid, water, straws, large sheets of paper.

Process:

Pour water into the builders' tray. You will not need to fill it completely. Add the colouring of your choice. (I have always found coloured inks to be very effective.) Add the washing up liquid and mix gently so that is distributed throughout the builders' tray. Get the children to blow through drinking straws to create a mass of bubbles. (N.B. Make sure that they blow, not suck – they will not like the taste!) When a large amount of bubbles have been made place a piece of paper over them and lift off. You will have an extra large bubble print. This can be used for a variety of purposes – display in their own right, as a background for children's pictures of other watery creatures, as covers for books, etc.

Further possibilities:

Just enjoy the bubble making –without taking prints.

Add liquid glycerine (available from chemists) to the water and colouring – does it make the bubbles last longer?

Blow down large pieces of tubing (readily available from DIY stores). Can you make some enormous bubbles?

Forever Blowing Bubbles

Resources:
Bubble mixture, bubble blowers, water, and magnifying glasses.

Process:
Blowing bubbles and watching them float away into the sky is always enjoyable – whatever your age. This activity is designed to capture a few bubbles so that they can be investigated more closely.

Pour water into the builders' tray. You might wish to fill it to just below the rim. As long as it is deep enough for the bubbles to float on, that will be sufficient. Get the children to blow bubbles across the tray so that they land on the water. This requires a reasonable amount of concentration, and will itself provide lots of opportunity for discussion.
Why do some bubbles burst and others don't?
Watch the bubbles as they glide across the water. What changes can you see – in shape, colour and size? What happens if the bubbles bump into each other? Can the children blow the bubbles form one side of the tray to the other?

Further possibilities:
Look at the bubbles through a magnifying glass. Can the children draw what they see?
Add food colouring or inks to the water – does it make any difference to how the bubbles look when they land on the water. Can the children catch a bubble on a bubble wand and transfer it to the water? Can they collect a bubble that has landed on the water and blow it away?

Marvellous Marbling

Resources:

Water, marbling inks or oily paints. For a cheaper home made version, try using dry powder colour with a little sunflower or other cooking oil. Mix until the powder has been absorbed by the oil. The longer you keep this, the better it becomes. Keep it in a screw top container and either shake it or mix it thoroughly every time you use it.

Process:

Fill the builders tray with clean cold water and drip a few drops of the oily paint onto it. (It is worth pausing at this point to allow the children time to observe what happens, and to talk about it.) Stir up any oily globules that form, or blow them to create swirling patterns. When you (and the children!) are happy with the pattern that has been made take a sheet of paper and drop it onto the water. Lift it off and there you will have your pattern.

Further possibilities:

Add vegetable oil to the water in the tray, and then add food colouring.
You will get a different effect to using the process above, but one that is equally effective.

Take repeated marbling prints from the same tray – what happens to the colours and patterns?
Try using a variety of coloured papers, and more than one coloured ink.

Monoprints

Resources:

Two printing rollers, one to be kept clean and dry, the other one for paint, a shallow paint dish, ready mixed paint or a water based printing ink and paper of a similar size to the builders tray. Black paper is very effective.

Process:

Roll paint or ink from the dish all over the builders' tray. Continue rolling so that the tray is covered with a smooth and even layer of colour.

Let the children draw a picture or make marks in the paint using their fingers. They can work individually, in pairs or threes, or collaborate in a larger group to encourage collaboration. Carefully lay a large piece of paper over the picture or design. Use the clean roller to roll over the piece of paper to create an even print. Lift the paper off carefully to reveal the picture. Re- roll the paint in the builders' tray for the next individual or group.

Further possibilities:

Use a variety of tools to draw in the layer of paint before making the monoprint. Try using an old pencil, a comb, and the end of a paintbrush, a piece of card or a glue spreader. Dabbing a sponge across the paint gently also creates an interesting textured background.

Activity 21

Puddles and Rain

Resources:
Some rainfall!

Process:
Left outside with nothing in it, the builders' tray makes the perfect home for your very own puddle.
You might like to take groups of children outside during a shower of rain so that they can watch what happens when rain hits the tray. Can they hear any noises? What can they see happening – what happens when the rain hits the tray – does the shape of the droplet change? How do these things change as the tray fills with water? Make sure that the children have the opportunity to watch drops of rainfall into the tray as it gets filled with water – watch the ripples. What happens when two sets of ripples meet each other?

Watch what happens to the puddle over a period of time. Where does the water go? As the puddle evaporates from the builders' tray, draw a chalk line around it so show how it is reducing in size. (This is of course dependent on having some warm weather following your rainstorm!) It would be worth comparing your builders' tray puddle to others in your outside area – on the pavement, on the grass, or on the gravel. What is the same? What is different?
If a cold spell of weather is predicted, then you could be lucky and end up with a frozen puddle!

Further possibilities:
If you collect two puddle in two trays, you might like to investigate how a puddle can be cleared up – which materials are most absorbent? What happens when you try to brush the water out of the tray – where does it go to when it lands on the ground? Why does it disappear from the ground around the tray and not from the tray itself?

Look in ''Out and About', collection of poems by Shirley Hughes for some lovely puddly poems to accompany these activities.
Cut puddle shapes from shiny paper, or foil. Get the children to look at their reflections in the puddle – draw or paint them on wet paper (chalks are lovely for this activity) cut them out and mount them on their own puddle shape.

After looking at the ripples in the puddle make paintings of concentric circles.

Activity 22

Cornflour

Resources:

Cornflour, water, glitter, food colouring, spoons, and lolly sticks.

Process:

Mix the cornflour and water together until it forms a yoghurt - like consistency. Allow the children to play with the resulting mixture – it is fascinating stuff. Encourage and value their observations and questions. Give them time to watch as the cornflour drips from their fingers – get them to describe how it feels and how it looks. Jog across the cornflour with two fingers; bang it with a spoon – what happens? Try stirring the cornflour; slowly and then quickly – what do you notice?

The potential of this activity can be further increased if you compare what happens when you jog your fingers across a shallow tray of water, or indeed bang a spoon on the water. Why do the children think there are differences in what happens?

Encourage them to make marks with the lolly sticks and spoons.

Can they write their name in the cornflour? Can they write all the letters of their name before the first one has disappeared?

This mixture is excellent for practising letters and numbers as none of the marks are permanent.

You could use a large sand timer to set the children a challenge – how many times can they write the number 7 (for example) before the sand timer runs out. (A 60 second timer is particularly useful for this activity)

Further possibilities:

Add food colouring and/or glitter to the cornflour mix to create added interest.

If you put two different colours of food colour in – say blue and yellow – then the children can watch the colours change as they mix and handle the cornflour.

Allow the cornflour to dry out (it will do so during the course of a warm day or overnight) – discuss the changes with the children, then ask them to think about how they might get it's original state.

Cornflour finger paint

Resources:
Cornflour, cold water, gelatine, boiling water, food colouring.

Process:
In a saucepan mix half a cup of cornflour with three-quarters of a cup of cold water to make a smooth paste. Soak one envelope of unflavoured gelatine in quarter of a cup of cold water and set aside.
Pour two cups of boiling water over the cornflour mixture and stir.
Put the cornflour mixture onto the stove and cook over medium heat, stirring constantly until the mixture boils and clears. Remove from the heat and stir in the gelatine. Cool.
Add a few drops of food colouring.
Spread in the builders' tray and allow the children to make marks with their fingers.

Further possibilities:
Try using other implements too – pieces of thick card, paint rollers, etc.
Put a selection of colours into the tray – look at what happens when they mix.

Cornflour modelling

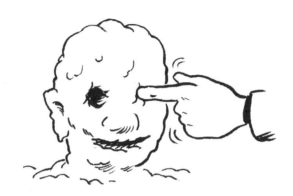

Cornflour Clay.
This clay can be air-dried and then painted.
Store any unused clay in an airtight container in the fridge.

Resources:
2 cups of salt
2/3 cup of water
1 cup of cornflour
_ cup of water

Process:
Put 2 cups of salt and two thirds of a cup of water into a saucepan, place on the stove and bring this to the boil. Add 1 cup of cornflour to two-thirds of a cup of water and mix well. Stir in the salt and water mixture. Knead it into clay.

Put the clay into the builders' tray and encourage the children to experiment with the material.
Resist the temptation to provide a large selection of tools, as this reduces the opportunity for children to handle the material.

Further possibilities:
Try giving the clay to the children while it is still warm from cooking.

Roads and Railways

Resources:
Large sheets of paper, toy cars, trains, construction equipment. Playmobil figures.

Process:
Cut out a large sheet of paper so that it fits neatly into the builders' tray. (You may wish to secure it to the tray with blue tack).

Let the children draw a road and railway system on the paper for use with the cars and trains. If you allow the children to do this unaided you will gain an insight into their understanding of the way that the three dimensional world can be represented in two dimensions. You might wish to draw a map of your immediate location for the children to use. Make sure that your setting is clearly represented. Show as many of the nearby roads as possible so that children can identify where they live and re enact their route to school/nursery/ playgroup in the morning.

Make the map come alive by encouraging the children to make buildings and trees with the constructing equipment or through junk modelling.

Look for aerial views of your setting on the Internet – these can be obtained at www.multimap.com   Laminate them so that the children can compare them with the representation created in the builder's tray.

Further possibilities:
Make maps of stories that you have read with the children –
Red Riding Hood, Goldilocks and The Three Bears,
We're Going on a Bear Hunt, Handa's Surprise, Rosie's Walk etc.

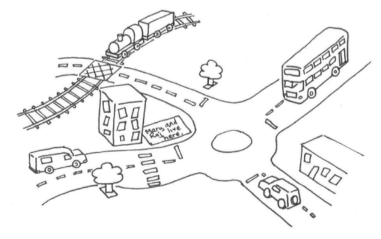

The Land of Ice and Snow

Resources:

Junk modelling materials – cardboard boxes, plastic pots, etc. Strong aluminium foil, cotton wool, blue foil paper. Toy polar bears, or penguins, Eskimo puppets – other examples of life in cold climates.

Process:

Cover the base of the builder's tray with blue foil. Arrange the boxes and pots on the tray so that they are stable. You might wish to pile some of them high into a mountain, and create some smaller separate structures to represent icebergs. If necessary glue some parts of the structure together, to increase stability. When you are happy with the structure, begin to cover it in aluminium cooking foil, smoothing it over the boxes and pots. Make sure that you cover the boxes and pots thoroughly. You may wish to glue the foil to some parts of the structure.

Add cotton wool snow, where you think appropriate.

Then, to bring the scene to life add toy animals and people; for example polar bears or penguins. Let the children explore and play with he small world.

Further possibilities:

You might like to read Penguin Small by Mink Inkpen, to the children, or the story of The Last Polar Bear. Add animals that represent characters from these books to your icy landscape so that children can re-enact the stories.

If the children use the small world to make stories offer them the opportunity to take photographs of significant parts in their stories. When the photographs are developed, they can add captions and you will have invaluable material for bookmaking.

Activity 27

Inter Galactic Adventures

Resources:
Newspaper, Modroc modelling material (or Plaster of Paris bandage, available from chemists), toy space vehicles, 'aliens' made or drawn by the children.

Process:
Screw up the newspaper and arrange it across the builders' tray. You do not need to cover the tray completely, but this crumpled newspaper will form the contours of your landscape. Arrange some newspaper to form crater like structures. (This will make the end result more like a planetary surface). Lay the Modroc over the newspaper so that it completely covers it. Use long pieces where possible. When you have covered the e newspaper and the flat surface of the builders' tray, spray the Modroc with water from a hand held plant sprayer. This is a good time to put finishing touches to the basic shape of your planet's surface. Allow the structure to dry. (Unless you have made the Modroc very wet, or it is very cold, it should dry overnight)

You can now treat the surface of the planet in a variety of ways. You may wish to varnish it with watered down PVA glue, to give a shiny finish. If you add glitter to this mixture you will create a magical effect. If you decide that a more mysterious inter galactic effect is required, then paint it with a vibrant colour. Don't forget to involve the children. The end result will be much more meaningful to them if they have been involved in creating it.

Further possibilities:
Make up stories about the planet. Make maps and guides. Send postcards home from outer space.

Ask the children to make space vehicles from the construction equipment to explore their planet.

Reflections and Ripples

Resources:
Water, mirrors of various descriptions, mirror tiles. (Some excellent ones are available from IKEA)

Process:
Cover the bottom of the builders' tray with mirrors – or just put one large mirror tile in.
Let the children look at their reflections. Change the surface of the water, blow gently,
stir, drop water in, and spray water across the surface.
What happens to the reflections?

Further possibilities:
Add food colouring or inks to the water – what happens to
the reflections then?
Place the tray outside on a cloudy day, or under tree – look
at these reflections.
What do the children notice?
Make drawings or paintings on wet paper to represent what
they see.

Activity 29

Five Little Speckled Frogs

Resources:
5 toy frogs (waterproof if you want to use water in the tray), water or blue foil, a log (large piece of bark makes an excellent log), pebbles, lily pads (available from aquatic centres and pet shops), grasses, etc. A laminated copy of the song Five Little Speckled Frogs, typed up on A4 paper.

Process:
If you have waterproof toy frogs, then pour water into the builders' tray. If not, then line the tray with blue foil paper. Add some grasses, pebbles and the lily pads to create a pond - like scene. Place the log to one side of the pool, and sit the five frogs upon it. Encourage the children to re-enact the rhyme, using the frogs to jump into the pool.

This activity provides many opportunities to develop mathematical understandings – counting and using the language of addition and subtraction are just two possibilities.

Further possibilities:
Add more frogs, to extend the challenge.

Hide some frogs under the lily pad – if there were five frogs to begin with, how many are hiding?

Add non-fiction books about the life cycle of the frog to the display.

Talk about ways of keeping cool.

Give the children the opportunity to use this activity outside – where you won't mind about them splashing the frogs about in the water.

Shaving Foam

Resources:
Shaving foam, glitter, a selection of play people and animals that live in cold climates.

Process:
Put several cans of shaving foam out with the builders' tray. (Non-allergenic types are readily available) Allow the children to experiment with making patterns by squirting the foam into the tray. Some children might like to make sculpture like structures, others might enjoy making trails across the tray.

Further possibilities:
Spray a large amount of shaving foam into the tray. Let children make marks, squiggles, write their names, practice letters and numbers.

Sprinkling glitter on the foam adds to the attraction of this resource. Offer magnifying glasses so that children can look closely at how the glitter is sparkling on the foam.

Add some penguins, or polar bear, or some play people and you will no doubt get some snowy stories to enjoy. Use the opportunity to explore the similarities and differences between shaving foam and real snow!

Activity 31

Building Sandcastles

Resources:
Damp sand, buckets, yoghurt pots, margarine tubs or various sizes, spades, shells, etc.

Process:
Because the builders' tray is nice and shallow, it is much easier for children to build sandcastles in, than the traditional deeper sand containers used in early years settings. Offer the children the opportunity to build sandcastles in the tray – working together as a group. Take photographs of the finished castles, to make a book. (This is very important, as the children will no doubt be reluctant to see their castle disappear to make way for the next one!) Allow the children to devise captions for their castle. They might like to give it a name, or say who lives there.

Further possibilities:
Let the children make flags for their castle, and add water for a moat if they want to. Unlike at the beach, the moat will not disappear! If you have a selection of play people available, then the children can decide on inhabitants for their castle and make up stories.

Activity 32

Using dry sand

Resources:
Dry sand, rakes, lolly sticks, jugs, funnels.

Process:
The dimensions of the builders' tray mean that it is easy for a group of children to work around it, either in collaboration, or engrossed in solitary play. Spread the dry sand over the builders' tray so that it is completely covered.
The children cam make tracks in the sand, with their fingers, rakes, lolly sticks, paintbrushes, cars, etc.
Provide containers to encourage pouring, sieving and funnelling. Encourage prediction – what will happen if?

Further possibilities:
If possible, have a wet sand activity nearby, so that the children have the opportunity to compare and contrast the same material in two different states. Which do they prefer? Why? Is wet/dry sand better for some activities than others? Why can't you build a sandcastle with dry sand?
For a change, put some old (but clean) socks and gloves out for the children to fill with dry sand. If possible you could tie the ends of the socks and gloves for the children, some of who might like to transform them into imaginary monsters while they play. This activity differs quite a different experience to filling rigid containers. Stick eyes or other features to the socks and gloves.
Put glitter in the sand – this makes it very exciting.
Sit a set of balancing scales in the middle of the tray along with a variety of containers, so that children can explore and experiment with weighing and balancing objects. The builders' tray will catch all the spillages.

Playdough

Resources:

Playdough in a variety of colours: add rice, herbs, lavender seeds and orange peel for interest.

Process:

Put the play dough in the tray, and allow the children to explore its texture. What can they find out about it? Hoe does it feel? Does it smell? What does it remind them of?

Resist the temptation to put out lots of implements to roll and cut with, as this reduces the opportunity for the children to handle the dough, lessening the sensory experience. It is also important to resist requests to 'make me a cat, dinosaur, puppy etc' Flattering and enjoyable as this may be for you, it means that children are constantly looking to emulate an adults achievements, and this is not appropriate. Better to offer them vocabulary to talk about their experiences, and to share in the word play that often ensues from this type of activity.

Further possibilities:

Use the playdough to develop a mathematical vocabulary, through encouraging the children to roll the dough out, or to change it's shape. Encourage them to mix doughs of different colours together – often this is frowned upon, and that's a shame, because learning opportunities are lost. How does the playdough change colour? Look at the marbled effect that occurs at the beginning of such mixing – what is happening?

More Playdough

Resources:
Playdough, matchsticks, lolly sticks, twigs, feathers, buttons, beads, sequins, etc.

Process:
Put the playdough and other modelling materials in the builders' tray. Encourage the children to make small lands with them. You will be amazed at the power of their imaginations. Allow them to work in pairs or small groups; whichever you think is most appropriate. Take photographs of their models. You may be able to carefully transfer them to a cork tile for display.

Put the photographs into a book with the children's comments or captions. This would be a nice volume to sit alongside your book of sandcastles, if you have tried Activity 31.

Further possibilities:
If you have been working with Maurice Sendak's Where The Wild Things Are then you might ask the children to make an island for a Wild Thing, or a palace for Max. You will find other similar possibilities in many children's stories. It is important to eave the activity open ended, so that there is room for the children's ideas.

Activity 35.

Robin Hood's Den

Resources:
A selection of miniature conifers, greengrocer's grass or moss, Robin Hood figures, toy woodland animals. (These could be Playmobil, or the children's own small drawings cut out and laminated). If you would like to add water to the environment you might use a shallow dish, or blue material, or crumpled foil. You could also use pebbles and gravel, for the shore beside the stream.

Process:
You might invite a group of children to help you set up this small world, so that they can be involved in placing the plants, moss and other features. If using moss, spread it over the base of the tray, leaving a space (perhaps about a quarter of the tray – but it really is up to you) for gravel and water. Place the trees so that a den is suggested – too spread out, and there will be nowhere for Robin to hide from the Sheriff.
Add the figures and let the children explore the small world, making stories and sharing ideas.
You might like to collect the stories and make a book 'The New Adventures of Robin Hood.' Add tension to the stories by leaving a Robin Hood 'Wanted' poster near your small world. What will the children do to help Robin?

Further possibilities:
Why not mirror this small world in your role-play area? Create Robin Hood's Den in your outdoor area. You might like to look at the appropriate page in Each Peach Pear Plum to give you and the children clues as to what he might have in there.

Using your marbles

Resources:

Marbles in a variety of colours and sizes and a marble run.

Process:

Because the builders' tray has a rim it is a very useful place for children to play with the marbles as there is less likelihood of them rolling all over the floor of your setting!

Even without the marble run, children can have an enjoyable time looking at and playing with the marbles. Keep a magnifying glass with this activity – marbles are fascinating things, often containing air bubbles – which look wonderful when magnified. Watch them rebound off the side of the tray – how many times can you make them do this before they stop?

Put the pieces of marble run in the tray. Who can build the longest or shortest run? Can the children find a way to measure how long it takes the marble to come down the run? Alternatively, can they use the marble run as a timer? How many times can they hop, write their name, sing Jack and Jill, etc, before the marble comes out of the run? Can they find a way to record what they have done?

Further possibilities:

You might like to line the sides of the tray with different materials. (They will attach easily with sticky tape, and are also easily removed). Try strips of bubble plastic, or foam, aluminium foil or polystyrene tiles cut into strips. What difference doe sit make to how the marbles behave, or the noises that they make?

Does changing the sides of the tray make playing with the marbles more or less exciting?

Having a sort out

Resources:
Collections of apparently random objects; stones, shells, buttons, keys, ribbons, seeds, tickets, beads, socks, etc.

Process:
Place a large selection of objects into the tray. Tell the children that they need sorting out. Let them sort the objects in their own way, and then discuss the reasons for their choices with them. Note how original the children are in their classifications, do not constrain them to labelling that adults might readily choose such as 'all the keys' or all large things, etc.'

Further possibilities:
You might also use this activity for counting, and encouraging the children to record what they have counted. Be open to their own innovative ways of recording. It will be important for the children to see a real purpose for their counting – for example you might want to say that 'We need to check that we have all the keys at the end of the day'.

Play a game with the children. Ask them to choose a small selection of objects that they think go together, and show them to the rest of the group. Can the children guess the connection?

Target Practice

Resources:
Chalks, or a piece of paper large enough to fit inside the builders' tray, beanbags.

Process:
Draw a simple target on the base of the builders' tray with chalk – if you wet the chalk before you draw, the colour will be thicker and clearer. Alternatively, place the plain paper into the try and draw a target on that. Use the target with beanbags either indoors or out. You might wish to assign simple numerical scores to the different coloured areas of the target, so that children can work out their score after say three throws.

Further possibilities:
Vary the way that you draw the target – instead of using the traditional concentric circles, you might divide the tray into quarters, or sixths, or divide it longwise.

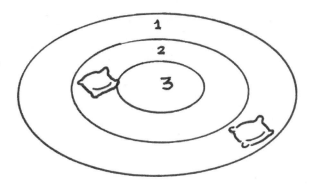

Activity 39

Opposites attract

Resources:
Magnets, including pairs of magnets, and a selection of objects, magnetic and non-magnetic. (Paper clips are a good thing to include)

Process:
Provide the children with magnets and the selection of objects. Let them explore the property of the magnets. Can they push one magnet from one side of the tray to another without touching it?
Can they make a long chain of paper clips hang from one magnet – just how long can they make it?
Encourage the children to articulate their ideas about what is happening. If you share their excitement in enquiry then you will help to build an atmosphere of enthusiastic curiosity.

Further possibilities:
Provide iron filings in transparent containers.
What happens when the children bring the magnet near to the container?

All wound up

Resources:
A collection of wind-up clockwork toys. Try and have a selection that show variations in movement – for example some that walk, others might jump, have wheels, or travel in a variety of directions.

Process:
Invite the children to investigate the toys to see what they might do. You might want to make sure that the children know how to wind the toys up without over winding them, so that they can use them independently of adult help.

Just watching the toys is fascinating for young children, and no doubt there will be much laughter as they wobble or drive their way round the tray. How do the children think that the toys work? Do they have anything at home that works by winding a key –maybe they night have a jewellery box, or clock for example.

Further possibilities:
Organise races between the toys. Which one can cross the builders' tray first? Which toy lasts the longest on one 'wind'?

Listen to the noises that the toys make. Can the children replicate these noises with any of the instruments available to them?

Try and have an object with a clockwork mechanism available for the children to disassemble. An old clock might be ideal for this purpose. Spread the pieces out in the builders' tray so that the children can have a closer look.

5 Ducks Went For a Swim One Day

Resources:

Water, five baby ducklings, one mother and one father. (The sort used at bath time is best, as they will float in the water) The words to Five Ducks went for a swim one Day, typed up and laminated, so that it can be used with water. An excellent book to have with this activity would be Five Little Ducks, by Ian Beck.

Process:

Pour water into the tray and add the ducks. If you wish to make it even more interesting you might add one or two plants that are happy to sit in water for a while around the edge. Grasses and reeds are ideal for this. If you have any lily pads (see Activity 29) then add these as well.

Float the ducks on the water, and let the children re-enact the song. If you have it typed up and laminated nearby they can sing it through together with their friends, and when an adult is present, then their attention can be drawn to the print. For example, getting the children to run their fingers under the words as they sing, etc.

Further possibilities:

Write about what you think happened to the baby ducks when they went 'over the hills and far away…'

Use the activity to develop counting skills, and the language of addition and subtraction.

Hide and Seek

Resources:

Sawdust, wood shavings, or straw and toy animals. Wood shavings are fascinating to use, and promote a lot of discussion in their own right.

N.B Make sure that you are aware of any children who might suffer from asthma, or who may be allergic to the straw or sawdust. Sterilised sawdust, sold as pet bedding in pet shops is cheap and widely available.

Process:

Fill the builders' tray with straw or sawdust, and bury the toy animals in it. Allow the children to come and find them, and then take the play in the direction that they wish. They might wish to continue to play hide and seek games with the animals, taking it in turns to hide them from each other, or they may wish to develop narrative play, pretending to feed the animals and maybe making homes for them.

Further possibilities:

Hide collections of things in the sawdust – keys, pebbles, shells, etc.
Play an odd one out game with the children. Hide a collection of objects that all have something in common – except for one. Can they find the odd one out? Can they create odd one out challenges for each other?

Activity 43

Construction equipment

Resources:
Lego, Duplo, Mobilo, Stickle Bricks, or Octagons – whichever construction equipment you are focussing on.

Process:
Whenever children use the construction equipment, they seem to need to spread it out and sort through it in order to choose the pieces that they will need to build their desired construction.

The builders' tray is an ideal way to contain this, as, because of the rim, pieces are less likely to spread all over the floor.

It also provides a stable surface for the children's models and a ready-made display space.

Children can work on individual models, or collaborate on building individual pieces that contribute to say a small town scene, with houses and a police station for example.

Further possibilities:
Line the builders' tray with gravel, or greengrocers grass and place the buildings on the new surface for added atmosphere.

Make a map, as suggested in Activity 25, put it in the tray and get the children make vehicles and buildings to use with it.

Encourage the children to make labels for their models. Encourage them to reflect on the models that they have made and to talk about what pleased them most.

Natural Sculpture

Resources:

Stones, twigs, pieces of driftwood, leaves, pieces of bark, etc. Any suitable natural materials will do. You might wish to have postcards, photographs books and magazines with pictures of sculptures available for the children to see.

Process:

Put a selection of materials in the builders' tray and encourage the children to firstly explore them, and then build with them. They might like to do this individually or in groups.

Be prepared for the children to make many changes to their sculpture before deciding that it is finished.

Allow time for other children in the setting to look at and comment on how the children have arranged their objects and which they have chosen to use.

If practical, you might like to leave one sculpture out for say, a week, and look at how it changes over a period of time.

Further possibilities:

Photograph the sculptures, so that you have a record of the children's work. If possible take the children to see some sculptures locally.

You could make some simple weaving frames with twigs and strings. Offer the children a selection of grasses and leave sin the builders' tray, and they will be able to weave with natural materials as well as sculpt with them.

Blow, blow, blow your boat

Resources:
Paper, card, scissors, glue, sellotape, paper clips, etc.

Process:
Set the children the challenge of making a little boat, or raft, that will sail from one side of the builders' tray to the other. They will need to experiment with various sizes of card and paper, and with ways of attaching a sail. They may like to draw and cut out a paper person to sail on their boat.

When they are happy with the craft that they have made let them blow it across the water.

Are there any other ways that they could propel their boat? A simple fan made from pleated paper would be one way to try. They might like to race their boats.

Further possibilities:
Make a book of boat designs.

Keep a Ship's Log of places that the little boats have visited.

Add rocks and pebbles to the builders' tray to create an obstacle course or maze for the boats.

Read The Little boat by Kathy Henderson to the children, it will give them many ideas for imaginary play.

Activity 46

Snow business

Resources:
Snow, and a certain amount of luck!

Process:
If you are lucky, and you have some snow during the winter months, then a builder's tray is perfect for catching some, and bringing it in doors. Leave the tray outside during snowy weather, and allow it to fill with snow. Take the children out of doors, and if the snow is reasonably thick, get them to collect snow to put in the tray.

Build a miniature snowman in the tray, adding features such as a face and a hat and scarf. And with the help of other adults in the setting, bring it indoors. Can any of the children predict what will happen? It would be a very good idea if you built him a twin brother outside, who is likely to last a whole lot longer! (This might prevent some upset on the part of the children)

Take photos of both snowmen over a period of time, and compare them.

These could be turned into a wall display, or a book.

Further possibilities:
Read The Snowman by Raymond Briggs to the children, and show them the video. You could make up a group story about the children's' own adventures with the snowman during shared writing sessions.

Make sure that you have magnifying glasses available, both indoors and out, so that the children can examine the snowflakes closely.

Washday Blues

Resources:
Washing powder, soap flakes, scrubbing brushes, and sponges, nail brushes, water, dirty doll's clothes, and a scrubbing board if you can obtain one!

Process:
Ask the children to come and wash the doll's clothes for you. They will need to lather up the washing powder or soap flakes. You might want to talk to them about how washing was done before the advent of washing machines.

There are lots of opportunities for scientific observations here. What I happening when they scrub the clothes? How do the dirty marks disappear? Does washing powder work best – or soap flakes? (You could have the chance to discuss the notion of fair testing with the children.) How can a washing machine clean the clothes if it doesn't scrub them? How are they going to rinse the clothes? How will they know that they have got rid of all the soap y water, and why would they want too?

Does cold or warm water work best?

Make sure that you provide a washing line so that the children can dry their clothes, when they have washed them.

Further possibilities:
Link to the story of 'Mrs Lather's Laundry' by Allan Ahlberg. The children could be inspired to wash lots of things for you! Make up your own version of 'Here we go round the Mulberry Bush'. This is the way we wash the clothes, scrub the clothes, rinse the clothes, etc. Take photographs of the children at play and turn it into a book.

Activity 48

Minibeast Land

Resources:
Compost, moss, grasses, bark, old dried leaves, rocks and pebbles, toy minibeasts – beetles, spiders, ants, etc.

Process:
Spread the compost over the base of the builders' tray. Position the grasses pebbles, leaves and moss to create a minibeast friendly environment. The addition of an old log or piece of bark adds to the authenticity. Add the minibeast and let the children explore the environment.

If you listen carefully to the children you will be able to ascertain what they already know about minibeast and their preferred environments, and through shared conversations offer them new vocabulary and answer the questions that arise whilst they are playing. This is a wonderful environment to create, it appeals to so many of the senses – the leaves and compost will smell (not unpleasantly) and there will be a variety of textures to explore.

It would be a wonderful way to bring the book 'In The Tall Tall Grass' to life, with children being able to think up noises for their own minibeasts to make.

Further possibilities:
Use the small world to write you own version of Dear Zoo. Instead of 'I wrote to the zoo to send me a pet…' You could write 'I wrote to the minibeast park to send me a…' It could continue with 'They sent me a spider. He was too tickly, I sent him back!' Make sure that you let the children contribute their ideas.

Giant Jigsaws

Resources:
Large sheets of paper or card – cut to fit the interior base of the builders' tray and a camera.

Process:
Work with small groups of children to paint a large image – it could be abstract or representational onto the large sheet of paper or card. Take a photograph of the finished product. (This is important as it is going to act as a guide for those doing the jigsaw)
When the finished artwork is dry, cut into an appropriate number of irregularly shaped pieces. If practical, you might wish to cover the pieces carefully with sticky backed plastic – this will make the jigsaw more robust.
Groups, pairs or individual children can work with the photograph of the original picture to do the jigsaw.

Further possibilities:
Make a collection of jigsaws made by the children so that they can develop favourites.
Use the builders trays as a place where children can complete commercially produced jigsaws, the pieces will be safely contained inside its' rim.
Scan children's pictures into the computer – print off and laminate, to make further child produced jigsaws.

Activity 50:

Down the drain!

Resources:
Pieces of guttering and drainpipe – readily available at DIY merchants, a water container on legs, jugs, small objects that will slide down the drainpipe.

Process:
Put the builders' tray in front of the 'off the floor' water container. Prop the piece of drainpipe or guttering so that one end is against the water tray and one end is in the builders' tray.

There are numerous possibilities for what could happen next. Pour water down the guttering so that it flows into the tray. What happens as the tray on the floor fills? Organise 'races' so that children pour water down a piece of guttering and a piece of drainpipe at the same time. Drop objects down the tubes – some of which will float and others that won't. Alter the angle of the pipes and gutters – what happens to the water flow?

Further possibilities:
You could carry out a similar activity using grain, dry sand or very small gravel instead of water.

Collect a selection of pipes that have bends, and pieces to join them with – can the children put them together so that they can transfer water from the water tub to the builders tray?

This would be a good activity to accompany work on Incey Wincey Spider.

CHILDREN'S BOOKS MENTIONED IN THE TEXT:

Dear Zoo Puffin Books; ISBN: 014050446X

Mrs. Lather's Laundry Puffin Books; ISBN: 0140312439

In The Tall Tall Grass Red Fox; ISBN: 0099131714

The Snowman Hamish Hamilton Children's Books; ISBN: 0241141036

5 Little Ducks : Orchard Books; ISBN: 1852134976

Each Peach Pear Plum : Viking Children's Books; ISBN: 0670287059

Where The Wild Things Are, Maurice Sendak: Red Fox; ISBN: 0099408392

Penguin Small: Mick Inkpen: Hodder Children's Books; ISBN: 034061935X

The Last Polar Bears Harry Horse: Puffin Books; ISBN 0140567127

We're Going On a Bear Hunt: Walker Books; ISBN: 0744523230

Handa's Surprise Eileen Browne: Walker Books; ISBN: 074455473X

Rosie's Walk: Red Fox; ISBN: 009941399X

Out and About: Shirley Hughes: Walker Books; ISBN: 0744560624 Reissue

One World: Michael Foreman Red Fox; ISBN: 0099834804

Sally and The Limpet: Simon James Walker Books; ISBN: 0744520207

Brown Bear, Brown Bear: Eric Carle Puffin Books; ISBN: 0140502963

Harry and The Bucketful of Dinosaurs: Ian Whybrow: Gulling Publishing; ISBN: 1862332053

Dinosaur Roar: Paul Stickland Puffin Books; ISBN: 0140557024

Saturday Night at The Dinosaur Stomp: Carol Diggory Shields, Walker Books; ISBN: 0744563453

Time Tunnel: Arthur L'Hommedieu Child's Play (International) Ltd; ISBN: 0859539288

Dinosaurs: Meredith Hooper, Bert Kitchen: Cambridge University Press; ISBN: 0521477913

The Little Boat: Kathy Henderson, Walker Books; ISBN 0763603708

We hope you have found this publication useful. Other titles in our **'Exciting Things To Do'** series are:

STORYLINES:	50 ideas for using large puppets, dolls and soft toys in early years settings.	1-903670-06-3
LET'S WRITE:	50 starting points for writing experiences.	1-903670-18-7
LET'S EXPLORE:	50 starting points for science activities.	1-903670-11-X
OUTSIDE:	50 exciting things to do outside.	1-903670-07-1
STORYBOXES:	50 exciting ideas for storyboxes.	1-903670-16-0
NURSERY RHYMES:	50 nursery rhymes to play with.	1-903670-23-3
PICTURE THIS:	50 ways to use a camera.	1-903670-22-5
PLANT AN IDEA:	50 exciting ways to use flowers, trees and plant life throughout the year.	1-903670-24-1
LET'S BUILD:	50 exciting ideas for construction play	1-903670-30-6
MATHS THROUGH STORIES:	50 exciting ideas for developing maths through stories	1-903670-53-5
SMALL WORLD RECIPE BOOK:	50 exciting ideas for small world play.	1-903670-39-X
LITERACY OUTDOORS:	50 exciting starting points for outdoor literacy experiences	1-903670-53-5

For further details of all our early years resources, visit our website:

www.educationalpublications.com